# TOWERING GIANTS AND OTHER TALL MEGASTRUCTURES

Ian Graham

QEB Publishing

Created for QED Publishing by Tall Tree Ltd
www.talltreebooks.co.uk
Editor: Rob Colson
Designers: Malcolm Parchment and Jonathan Vipond
Illustrations: Apple Illustration and Caroline Watsonw

Published in the United States by
QEB Publishing, Inc.
3 Wrigley, Suite A
Irvine, CA 92618

www.qed-publishing.co.uk

A CIP record for this book is available from the
Library of Congress.

ISBN 978 1 60992 094 4

Printed in China

**Picture credits**
(t=top, b=bottom, l=left, r=right, c=centre)
**Alamy**: 6-7 Michael Doolittle/Alamy, 8 kpzfoto, 12 DBURKE; **Corbis** 11t Joel W. Rogers,
11b Joel W. Rogers, 17 Sean Aidan, Eye Ubiquitous/CORBIS, 22-23 Jose Fuste Raga/
CORBIS, 24-25 pix2go; **Creative Commons**19t Joi Ito, 22 Ratsbew, 23 Trubshaw, 27 Statoil;
**Dreamstime** 10 Stuart Pearcey; **Getty images** 9 Science & Society Picture, 13 Getty
Images, 18t Bloomberg, 18b Barcroft Media, 19b AFP; **istockphoto** 4-5 Mlenny
Photography; **Shutterstock** 8-9 Shutterstock, 12-13 Cupertino, 14-15 WH Chow, 14 Jessmine,
15 Songquan Deng, 16 Henryk Sadura, 18-19 Philip Lange, 20-21 Elena Yakusheva, 20
Alexander Chaikin, 24 Rorem, 28-29 Shutterstock, 28 Bart J

Words in **bold** are explained in the Glossary on page 32.

# Contents

# Aiming high

People have been fascinated by the construction of tall structures for thousands of years. Buildings that made everyone look skywards inspired awe and emphasized a ruler's wealth and power. Today, the tallest buildings are still expressions of wealth and power. They become famous and they make the places where they are built famous, too.

## Where are they built?

The tallest buildings are very expensive to construct, so they are usually built in the wealthiest parts of the world. For most of the 20th century, the world's tallest buildings were built only in North America. By the 1990s, countries such as Malaysia and Taiwan were building record-breaking skyscrapers. As China became wealthier in the 1990s and early 2000s, new skyscrapers were built in Chinese cities including Shanghai, Nanjing, Guangzhou, and Shenzhen. Today, the astonishing 2717-foot (828-meter) Burj Khalifa in Dubai, UAE, is the world's tallest skyscraper.

## Why are they built?

Skyscrapers are built for practical reasons as well as for fame. Land in big cities is very expensive. By building upwards instead of spreading out across the ground, skyscrapers have a small **footprint** (the area of land they occupy), but they pack a lot of homes, hotel rooms, and offices into this small area. The tallest towers are useful in other ways, too. They send radio and television signals over hills and tall buildings.

## MEGA FACTS

The world's first skyscraper was the Home Insurance Building in Chicago. It was built in 1885 and was 10 stories high. It was demolished in 1931.

4

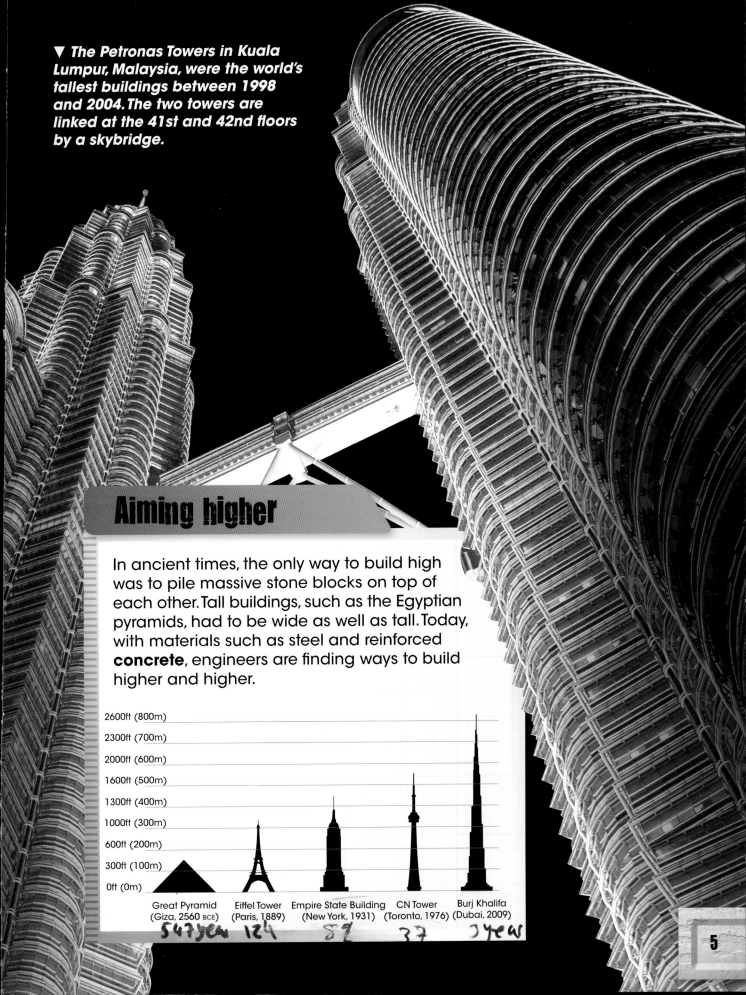

▼ *The Petronas Towers in Kuala Lumpur, Malaysia, were the world's tallest buildings between 1998 and 2004. The two towers are linked at the 41st and 42nd floors by a skybridge.*

## Aiming higher

In ancient times, the only way to build high was to pile massive stone blocks on top of each other. Tall buildings, such as the Egyptian pyramids, had to be wide as well as tall. Today, with materials such as steel and reinforced **concrete**, engineers are finding ways to build higher and higher.

2600ft (800m)

2300ft (700m)

2000ft (600m)

1600ft (500m)

1300ft (400m)

1000ft (300m)

600ft (200m)

300ft (100m)

0ft (0m)

Great Pyramid (Giza, 2560 BCE)

Eiffel Tower (Paris, 1889)

Empire State Building (New York, 1931)

CN Tower (Toronto, 1976)

Burj Khalifa (Dubai, 2009)

# Superstructures

The part of a skyscraper or tower that is above the ground, called the **superstructure**, is supported by another part hidden under the ground, called the **substructure**. The substructure stops the building from sinking into the ground, and also helps to prevent the whole structure from falling over.

## Supporting the weight

The weight of a house is held up by its walls. They are called **load-bearing walls**. If a skyscraper had load-bearing walls, they would have to be so thick that they would fill the base of the building. Instead, a skyscraper is held up by a frame that is usually made of steel. Thin walls, called **curtain walls**, hang from the building's frame like curtains.

## The first skyscrapers

The 16-story Monadnock Building in Chicago was one of the world's first skyscrapers. The northern half of the building was built using load-bearing walls, which are nearly 6.5 feet (2 meters) thick at the base. The southern half of the building was built using a steel frame and curtain walls like a modern skyscraper. The thin curtain walls create more space inside, especially on the first floor.

▶ Inside a skyscraper there is a strong frame. It supports the building's weight so that the walls can be very thin.

# Underground legs

A skyscraper or tower stands on a small base, like a pencil standing on end. A pencil falls over very easily, but skyscrapers and towers must not topple. To stop this happening, they are anchored to concrete and steel legs, called **piles**, that extend deep underground. The piles rest on solid rock or a concrete platform. This supports the building's weight and stops it from sinking. The piles also work like a tree's roots to hold the building upright. If the building tries to lean over, the ground grips the piles and holds it steady.

▶ Piles sit on the hard rock beneath the soil or on a specially constructed concrete platform.

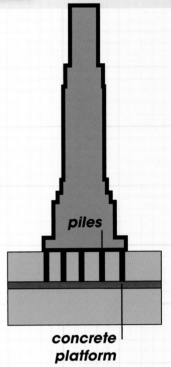

piles

concrete platform

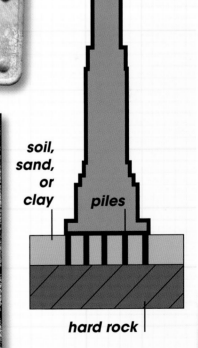

soil, sand, or clay

piles

hard rock

## MEGA FACTS

The Willis Tower in Chicago was the world's tallest skyscraper when it was completed in 1974. It is 1,450 feet (442 meters) high and weighs 226,070 tons (222,500 tonnes).

7

# Standing up to nature

Once a skyscraper is built, it has to withstand everything that nature throws at it. It might face hurricane-strength winds or shaking caused by an earthquake. Engineers use models, test rigs, and computer programs to ensure that wind and shaking will not cause problems.

## The big blow

To withstand the pressure, or pushing force, of the wind, today's super-tall skyscrapers have to be 50 times stronger than a 200-foot (60-meter) building of the 1940s. Model skyscrapers are placed in wind tunnels to study how the wind blows around them and to measure the wind pressure on the walls and windows. Computer models are used to show how the building bends and shakes, and to spot any weaknesses in the structure.

## Wind tunnel testing

This model of a skyscraper and the buildings around it was built to be placed in a wind tunnel for testing. The model is on a turntable, which can be rotated to study the effects of wind blowing from different directions.

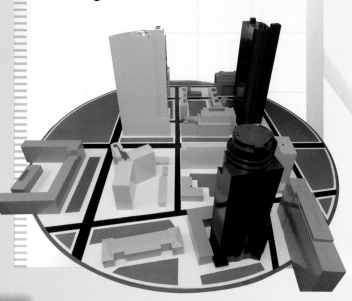

▼ **This massive ball is the 728-ton (660-tonne) tuned mass damper in Taipei 101, a skyscraper in Taiwan.**

# Shakin' all over

When the John Hancock Tower was built in Boston in the 1970s, it swayed and twisted in the wind much more than expected. The swaying and twisting motions were happening in time with each other. This is called **resonance**, and it can make a building shake dangerously. One way to protect a building from resonance is to use a **tuned mass damper**. This is a heavy chunk of metal that can move from side to side. When the building sways in one direction, the damper moves in the opposite direction, tugging the building back and stopping it from swaying too much. Tuned mass dampers and 1,500 tons (1360 tonnes) of steel beams, called braces, cured the John Hancock Tower's swaying.

▶ *Taipei 101's tuned mass damper hangs from the building's 92nd floor down to the 88th floor.*

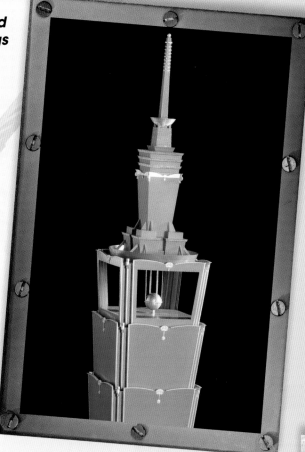

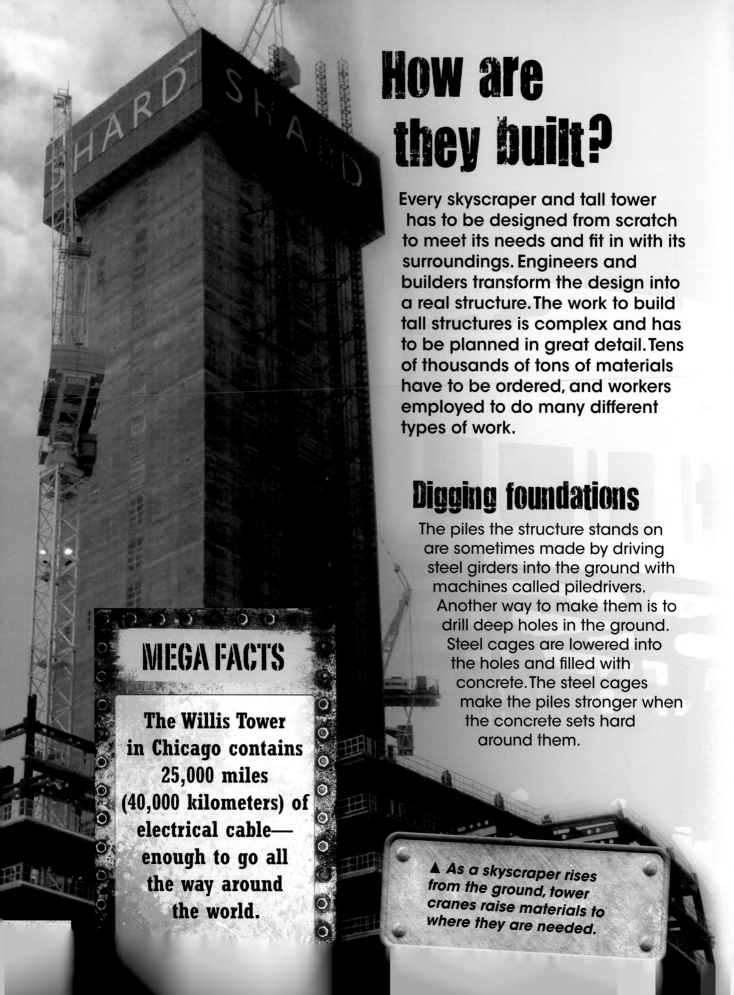

# How are they built?

Every skyscraper and tall tower has to be designed from scratch to meet its needs and fit in with its surroundings. Engineers and builders transform the design into a real structure. The work to build tall structures is complex and has to be planned in great detail. Tens of thousands of tons of materials have to be ordered, and workers employed to do many different types of work.

## Digging foundations

The piles the structure stands on are sometimes made by driving steel girders into the ground with machines called piledrivers. Another way to make them is to drill deep holes in the ground. Steel cages are lowered into the holes and filled with concrete. The steel cages make the piles stronger when the concrete sets hard around them.

## MEGA FACTS

The Willis Tower in Chicago contains 25,000 miles (40,000 kilometers) of electrical cable— enough to go all the way around the world.

▲ As a skyscraper rises from the ground, tower cranes raise materials to where they are needed.

# Floors and walls

The floors are made by laying steel panels, called **decking**, between the beams. Concrete is poured on the decking to make the floors. The exterior wall panels are attached to the outside of the building's frame. A crane lifts them into position and workers bolt them in place.

▶ *Workers have laid out decking to make a floor in this skyscraper. Now they are pouring concrete on top and leveling it.*

## Framing up

The building's steel frame is built on top of the piles. The frames of older buildings, such as the Empire State Building in New York City were held together using iron pins called **rivets**. Since the 1950s, skyscraper frames have been bolted or **welded** together.

## Finishing touches

Once the frame has been completed, there is still a vast amount of work to be done. The electrical cabling, lighting, plumbing and air conditioning have to be installed. The interior walls, and ceilings have to be fitted, too.

▼ *A welder welds parts of a skyscraper's steel frame together. He wears a visor to protect his eyes from the bright flames.*

The building's steel frame was finished in September 2007 and the **cladding** (outside covering) was completed by June 2008. The Shanghai World Financial Center opened on August 28, 2008.

▲ *The cladding panels were lifted into position by two tower cranes.*

In the 1990s, a new skyscraper was planned for Shanghai, China. The Shanghai World Financial Center was to be 1,510 feet (460 meters) high, making it the world's tallest building.

Construction began in 1997 then stopped due to a shortage of money. It started again six years later but the delay meant that by the time the building was finished, Taipei 101 in Taiwan had become the world's tallest building at 1,667 feet (508 meters) high. Plans were made to change the design of the Shanghai skyscraper so that it would be higher than Taipei 101, but the tallest it could go was 1,614 feet (492 meters).

# Shanghai World Financial Center

height: 1614 feet (492 m)

▼ The original design for the Shanghai World Financial Center was a tall, graceful, tapering tower with a circular hole at the top.

## Changing shape

The hole near the top was originally designed to be round, but this was thought to look too much like the Japanese flag, so it was changed to an angular shape.

▲ The Shanghai World Financial Center has 101 floors above ground and three floors below ground.

# Famous giants

There are thousands of skyscrapers, towers, and other tall structures all over the world. Some of them are so distinctive that they are instantly recognizable. The Great Pyramid, the Leaning Tower of Pisa, and the Empire State Building are among the world's most famous tall structures. Between them, they span 4,500 years of history.

## The Great Pyramid

Built at Giza in Egypt in about 2,560 BCE as a tomb for Pharaoh Khufu, the Great Pyramid was the world's tallest artificial structure for 4,000 years. It stands 480 feet (140 meters) high and the base is 755 feet (230 meters) long on each side. It was built from 2.3 million stone blocks weighing up to 15 tons (13.6 tonnes) each. It was originally clad in white limestone, but this was later stripped away and used to build other tombs or temples.

## The Leaning Tower of Pisa

This famous leaning tower was built in Pisa, Italy, in the 12th century. It started sinking on one side, and leaning over, when it was only three floors high. Over the centuries, there were several attempts to stop it leaning further, but they all failed. Then in 1998, soil was removed from beneath the non-sinking side of the tower. This straightened up the tower a little and saved it from collapsing.

▼ At the top, the Leaning Tower of Pisa leans nearly 13 feet (4 meters) from the vertical.

▼ *The Great Pyramid of Giza is the only one of the Seven Wonders of the Ancient World still standing.*

The Empire State Building was built in New York City in 1931. It was the first building to use the fast-track construction method that is used today. To save time and cut costs, work began while the building was still being designed. It was built around a strong central core containing the elevator shafts. The outside of the building is covered with limestone and stainless steel. It was built in just 410 days and at 1,250 feet (381 meters) high, excluding the spire, it was the tallest building in the world for 41 years.

spire

▶ *The Empire State Building was designed with an airship terminal at the top. The plan was for passenger airships to tie up to the 203-foot (62-meter) spire. However, strong winds blowing up the side of the building made it too dangerous so the terminal was canceled.*

## MEGA FACTS

From 1930 to 1931, three skyscrapers were built in New York City: first came 40 Wall Street, then the Chrysler Building, and finally the Empire State Building.

▼ The observation deck is located on the 124th floor, about two-thirds of the way up. Two high-speed elevators carry visitors up to the deck in just three minutes.

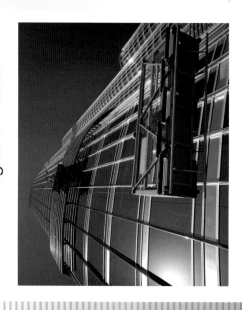

## Glass cladding

The superstructure is covered with a metal and glass cladding. Its 24,830 glass panels had to be cut to size by hand. The cladding has to be able to stand up to the extreme daytime heat and cooler nights of Dubai.

▲ As it neared completion, the finishing touches were made to the cladding by workers in special moving platforms called gondolas.

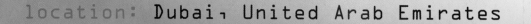

location: Dubai, United Arab Emirates

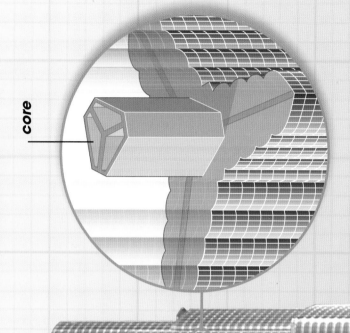

▼ *The Burj Khalifa's Y-shaped cross-section was inspired by a desert flower called hymenocallis.*

core

observation deck

# Burj Khalifa

The shimmering silver skyscraper Burj Khalifa in Dubai is by far the world's tallest building. It is so tall that it casts a shadow on clouds that glide below its glistening steel spire.
It contains homes for 25,000 people, plus a hotel, shops, and offices. Work on the building's superstructure began in March 2005 and was completed in 2009.

Unlike most skyscrapers, Burj Khalifa has a concrete internal structure instead of a steel frame. A steel frame would have made the building too expensive. It would also have made the tall, slender building too flexible—it would have swayed too much in the wind.

Burj Khalifa's Y-shaped design is called a buttressed core. The shape of the core provides torsional stability, which means that it resists twisting forces caused by the wind. The wings buttress (support) the core and each other.

height: 2717 feet (828 m)

# Skyscrapers

The first skyscrapers were built in the 1880s in Chicago. They were about 10 floors high, but skyscrapers have been getting taller and taller ever since. The height of modern skyscrapers and towers presents many engineering problems. Imagine having to take the stairs to your apartment or office on the 60th floor every day! The skyscrapers and towers that have shaped modern cities might never have been built if the elevator had not been invented. Cleaning windows hundreds of feet (meters) above the ground presents another major problem.

## MEGA FACTS

Using 18 cleaning cradles, it takes a team of people four months to clean the whole exterior of Burj Khalifa, the world's tallest skyscraper.

## Cleaning windows

Skyscrapers are covered with thousands of windows and all of them have to be cleaned. Window cleaners often work in cradles hanging down from a skyscraper's roof. The cleaner can move the cradle up, down, and sideways, to reach all the windows. Today, robot window cleaners are beginning to take over some of this work.

◀ *Skyscraper window cleaners need a good head for heights as they hang down outside the building, sometimes hundreds of feet (meters) above the ground.*

# Going up

The first public passenger elevator was installed in Haughwout's Department Store in New York City in 1857. As skyscrapers become taller and taller, their elevators have to move faster and faster to stop journeys up and down the building taking too long. The fastest skyscraper lifts travel at more than 35 miles per hour (60 kilometers per hour).

# Heating and cooling

A skyscraper's windows do not open to let in fresh air, so air has to be pumped through the building. The air is heated or cooled to maintain a comfortable temperature. A lot of equipment is needed to supply the air and also the water and waste removal services. For about every 10 floors of offices or apartments, a whole floor is set aside for equipment. These are called mechanical floors.

◄ *The elevators on the Lloyd's Building in London, UK, run up and down outside the building.*

▲ The lower floors up to level eight are taken up by a luxury hotel designed by the Italian fashion designer Giorgio Armani.

## MEGA FACTS

Residents and workers can make their way up and down Burj Khalifa by means of 57 elevators, eight escalators, and 2909 stairs.

The concrete structure was built first. It is strengthened with 34,600 tons (31,400 tonnes) of steel bars (left). After it was completed, the glass and steel cladding were fitted around the concrete (right).

## Water supplies

A giant building needs an enormous amount of water for its occupants. Burj Khalifa's water system distributes 250,000 gallons (946,000 liters) of water through the building each day. It comes from desalination plants that convert seawater into fresh water.

## Air conditioning

The tower is so tall that the temperature outside it is 12 degrees Fahrenheit (7 degrees Celsius) lower at the top than at the base. This air is sucked into the building to help cool it, using a technique called "skysourcing.".

By the time the cladding was added to the outside, Burj Khalifa was taller than two Empire State Buildings stacked on top of each other.

# Mighty monuments

Monuments are structures built to remember people or events. They may be statues, columns, tombs, temples, or other permanent structures. Two of the most instantly recognizable monuments are the Statue of Liberty in New York City and the Eiffel Tower in Paris, France.

▼ Just 240 visitors per day are allowed to climb the stairs to the Statue of Liberty's crown.

## The Eiffel Tower

The Eiffel Tower was built as a monument to the French Revolution. It was completed in 1889. At a height of 1024 feet, (312 meters) it was the world's tallest man-made structure. Today, communications **antennae** have raised its height to 1063 feet (324 meters). It was constructed from 18,038 pieces of iron. Its designer, Gustave Eiffel, was one of the first people to realize the importance of wind forces on tall structures. He designed the tower as an open lattice through which the wind could blow.

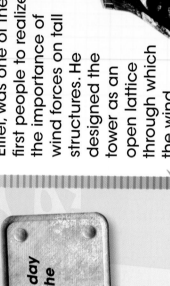

▲ The Eiffel Tower's iron structure is protected from rusting by paint. It is repainted every seven years. The job takes 25 painters more than a year and needs 65 tons (60 tonnes) of paint.

# The Statue of Liberty

The Statue of Liberty stands on Liberty Island in New York Harbor. Before air travel, when people crossed the Atlantic Ocean by ship, it welcomed tourists and immigrants arriving in New York City. It was a gift to the USA from France as a monument to freedom and democracy. With its stone base, it stands 305 feet (93 meters) high. It was made of copper sheets fixed to an iron tower. The tower was connected to the copper skin by an **armature**—a flexible framework that lets the skin move in strong winds without cracking. The statue was built in France in 1884, then taken apart and shipped to New York. It was reassembled on the stone base in 1886.

▲By the 1980s, the armature supporting the Statue of Liberty's skin had corroded and needed to be replaced.

## MEGA FACTS

The sunlit side of the Eiffel Tower expands more than the shaded side, making the top of the tower lean up to 7 inches (18 centimeters) away from the Sun.

# Masts and towers

In past centuries, towers were built as defensive structures or to hold church bells high above the ground. Much taller towers are built today for long-distance communications. Radio signals have to be broadcast over long distances. This is done by transmitters on top of tall masts or towers.

## Radio masts

**Radio masts** are usually made of an open lattice. The lattice is lighter than solid metal and it lets the wind blow through it. Unlike tall buildings, radio masts do not have any foundations under the ground to hold them upright. Instead, they are held up by cables called **guys** or metal rods called **stays**—just like the ropes that hold up tents.

*◄ The KVLY-TV mast in North Dakota is the world's tallest mast. It is made of a 1,948 feet (594-meter) steel lattice mast with a 112-feet-high (43-meter) transmitting antenna on top. When it was completed in 1963, it was the first artificial structure to exceed 2,000 feet (609 meters).*

*► The Sky Tower in Auckland, New Zealand, is a communications tower that can withstand winds of up to 125 miles per hour (200 kilometers per hour).*

# Towers

Cities need radio antennae high above the ground because tall buildings often get in the way of radio and television signals. Radio masts may not be very pretty to look at, but they are usually located in remote places where their appearance does not matter. They are not suitable for use in cities because their guys and stays take up too much land. Sometimes, in cities, radio antennae are fixed to the tops of tall buildings, but if this is not possible, a communications tower is needed. Concrete towers are used, because they look better than masts and they are self-supporting—they do not need guys or stays to hold them up.

## Tourist attractions

Concrete communications towers often have observation decks and restaurants near the top. The 1,814-foot (553-meter) CN Tower in Toronto, Canada, is the tallest concrete communications tower in the western hemisphere. At 1,076 feet (328 meters), the Sky Tower in Auckland, New Zealand, is the tallest in the southern hemisphere. The world's tallest concrete communications tower is the Canton Tower in Guangzhou, China, which stands 2,000 feet (610 meters) high. It was completed in 2010 in time to relay television pictures of the Asian Games. It is made of an open steel lattice wrapped around a strong concrete core.

▶ *The Canton Tower in Guangzhou, China, contains radio and television transmitters, observation decks, revolving restaurants, shops, and cinemas.*

## MEGA FACTS

The KVLY-TV mast was built in 1963 in just 30 days. At 2,060 feet (628 meters), it was the world's tallest artificial structure until Burj Khalifa was built.

# The CN Tower

In the early 1970s, a number of skyscrapers were built in Toronto, Canada's biggest city. These new buildings made it difficult for people to receive radio and television programs as they blocked the signal. The CN Tower was built in the middle of the city to broadcast signals from above the other buildings. It is one of the world's tallest towers. From the ground to the tip of its antenna, it stands 1814 feet (553 meters) high.

## What a view!

The CN Tower opened to the public in 1976. Up to two million people visit it every year. They travel up the tower in elevators and visit two levels called pods near the top—the Main Pod and an even higher Sky Pod. The Main Pod has a revolving restaurant that makes a complete rotation every 72 minutes. There are also observation decks giving views across the city. Brave visitors to one of the observation decks can stand on a glass floor and see the ground 1,122 feet (342 meters) below their feet!

▲ On a clear day, the view from the top of the CN Tower stretches to the horizon more than 100 miles (160 kilometers) away.

revolving restaurant

mechanical floors

open-air platform

microwave transmitter

## Building a giant

Construction work began in 1973. Most of the tower is made from concrete with a tall steel mast on the top. A six-sided pillar in the middle is surrounded by three massive supporting legs. The legs hold the tower steady in the strongest winds.

## Finishing off

The concrete construction work was completed by March 1975. The 335-foot (102-meter) steel antenna was lifted to the top in 44 pieces by a helicopter. The final section was bolted in place on April 2, 1975. The tower was opened to the public on June 26, 1976.

▼ *The tower's three-legged shape was produced by pouring concrete into a mold.*

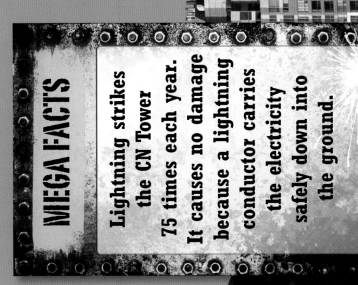

## MEGA FACTS

Lightning strikes the CN Tower 75 times each year. It causes no damage because a lightning conductor carries the electricity safely down into the ground.

# Offshore platforms

Offshore platforms stand in the sea and bring valuable oil and natural gas up from below the seabed. The part of an offshore platform that is above the waves is enormous, but the part that is under the sea is much, much bigger, and the whole structure is as tall as a skyscraper.

The tallest platforms are the ones that stand on the seabed on legs made of steel or concrete. Several decks of equipment and crew quarters, called the topsides, sit on top of the legs. The platform is towed out to sea and then tanks inside the legs are flooded so that they sink to the seabed. Only about 100 feet (30 meters) or so of the legs are visible above the waves.

▲ *Offshore oil platforms are made on land and then towed out to sea.*

# Record breaker

The biggest and heaviest structure ever transported is the Troll A gas platform. It stands in the sea about 50 miles (80 kilometers) northwest of Bergen, Norway, bringing natural gas up from the Troll gas field. Its giant concrete legs are 1,210 feet (369 meters) high and weigh an astonishing 723,000 tons (656,000 tonnes). Troll A was built in the sheltered waters of a Norwegian fjord. When the legs were completed, they were partly submerged so that the decks could be lifted on top. Then the whole structure, now 1,549 feet (472 meters) high, was towed out to its current position and sunk to the seabed. The massive legs buried themselves 115 feet (35 meters) into the soft mud.

▼ **The Eiffel Tower was once the world's tallest man-made structure. The Troll A offshore platform is 525 feet (160 meters) taller.**

◄ **This oil platform is designed to drill in water depths of up to 9,800 feet (3,000 meters).**

# Failures and accidents

Tall structures are designed to be safe and built with great care, but sometimes something may go wrong. Although this is very rare, tall structures can suffer extraordinary accidents, failures, and faults that their designers and builders had not anticipated. The tallest skyscrapers are covered with tens of thousands of windows. It is vital that they do not break or fall out. Large, heavy panels of glass falling from a skyscraper into the streets below could be lethal.

## Falling windows

When the John Hancock Tower in Boston was built in the 1970s, it was covered with blue, mirrored glass. Soon after the windows were installed, they started crashing to the ground. Researchers found that the **solder** (a metal **alloy**) that filled the space between the glass and frame was too stiff. When the panels flexed in the wind, as they were designed to do, the solder cracked. This cracked the glass and the windows fell out.

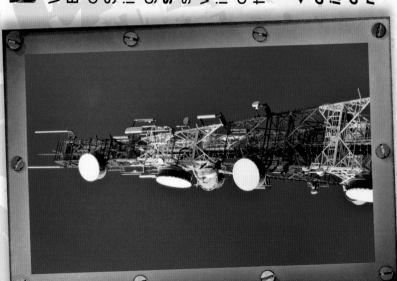

▼ *Dozens of radio masts have fallen down over the years. Most toppled in storms, while some were hit by airplanes. Others collapsed during maintenance work.*

▶ All 10,344 windows of the John Hancock Tower in Boston had to be replaced when a design fault was discovered.

# Safety first

It is important that workers use safe building methods to prevent serious accidents. On June 27, 2009, a nearly finished 13-story apartment building in Shanghai, China, fell onto its side. An inquiry found that the problem was caused by workers digging a deep pit for an underground garage on one side of the building while also piling earth high on the other side. These earth movements unbalanced the ground so much that it gave way.

▲ This building in Shanghai, China, fell because of nearby digging. Its foundation piles stuck out of its base like the roots of a fallen tree.

# Looking into the future

Architects, designers, and engineers continue to develop skyscrapers and towers in shapes that have never been seen before. Some new designs for tall structures are driven by function. Others unashamedly seek the biggest "wow" factor and the sharpest intake of breath from visitors.

## The Gherkin

The 590-foot (180-meter) building in London, UK, called 30 St Mary Axe, better known as the Gherkin, is egg-shaped. The architects Norman Foster and Ken Shuttleworth gave it its curved shape in order to encourage the wind to flow around it. The wind is not deflected downwards, so the building does not create blasts of wind on the pavements below as other skyscrapers can.

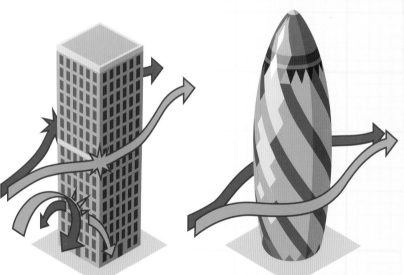

▲ Skyscrapers with flat sides can deflect winds down onto pedestrians at street level. The Gherkin's shape allows wind to flow around it.

▶ The Capital Gate skyscraper in Abu Dhabi is supported by an external frame of diagonal supports, called a diagrid.

# Shaping up

Until recently, most skyscrapers were rectangular blocks. Now, though, more architects and engineers are exploring the possibilities of building skyscrapers in all sorts of different shapes. The 525-foot ( 160 meter) Capital Gate building in Abu Dhabi, UAE, leans at a precarious angle of 18 degrees. Unlike the Leaning Tower of Pisa, the Capital Gate building was designed to have this distinctive lean. Its floors overhang each other from the 12th floor upwards.

Even stranger-looking skyscrapers are being planned. Future skyscrapers may change shape as their floors slowly rotate around the building's core. A 1,380-foot (420-meter) skyscraper like this is planned for Dubai. Each floor will rotate separately from all the others. The building's energy needs will be met by its own wind turbines and solar panels.

▼ *The Pearl River Tower in Guangzhou, China, lets air flow through it, powering wind turbines inside the building. The air is fed into the turbines through funnel-like openings in the building's walls.*

## MEGA FACTS

The Pearl River Tower in Guangzhou, China, may be the first "green" skyscraper. As well as wind turbines, it has solar panels and other green technology.

# Glossary

**alloy**
A mixture of a metal and one or more other elements. Steel is an alloy of iron and carbon.

**antennae**
The parts of a radio that transmit or receive radio signals.

**armature**
A framework that holds up a sculpture or statue.

**cladding**
A building's outer protective covering, usually not load-bearing.

**concrete**
A construction material made of sand, gravel, cement, and water. Reinforced concrete is strengthened by adding steel mesh or wires.

**curtain wall**
A type of exterior wall used in the construction of skyscrapers. It hangs from the frame and does not bear any weight.

**decking**
Metal sheets that are covered with concrete to make a building's floors.

**footprint**
The area of the ground taken up by a building.

**guy**
A wire or cable that anchors a radio mast to the ground.

**load-bearing wall**
Any wall that bears part of the weight of a building.

**pile**
A column buried in the ground to hold a building upright.

**radio mast**
A tall structure, usually made of steel, with radio antennae at the top.

**resonance**
The tendency of an object to vibrate more and more violently at certain frequencies.

**rivet**
An iron or steel pin with a wide head at one end, used to fasten steel girders together.

**solder**
An alloy that is used to fuse (join) two metallic parts together.

**stay**
One of the rods used to anchor a radio mast to the ground.

**substructure**
The foundations of a tall building, which support it and hold it upright.

**superstructure**
The part of a tall building that is above the ground.

**tuned mass damper**
A heavy weight that stops a building from swaying dangerously by moving in the opposite direction.

**welded**
When metal or plastic parts are joined by melting the edges where they meet so that they run together and set as they cool.

# Top 10 tallest skyscrapers

| Skyscraper | Location | Height |
|---|---|---|
| 1. Burj Khalifa | Dubai, UAE | 2,717 ft (828m) |
| 2. Taipei 101 | Taipei, Taiwan | 1,667 ft (508 m) |
| 3. Shanghai World Financial Center | Shanghai, China | 1,614 ft (492 m) |
| 4. International Commerce Center | Hong Kong, China | 1,588 ft (484 m) |
| 5. Petronas Towers | Kuala Lumpur, Malaysia | 1,483 ft (452 m) |
| 6. Greenland Financial Center | Nanjing, China | 1,476 ft (450 m) |
| 7. Willis Tower | Chicago, USA | 1,450 ft (442 m) |
| 8. International Finance Center | Guangzhou, China | 1,444 ft (440 m) |
| 9. Jin Mao Tower | Shanghai, China | 1,381 ft (421 m) |
| 10. Two International Finance Center | Hong Kong, China | 1,362 ft (415 m) |

# Take it further

Think about the materials used to build skyscrapers and towers. Why do you think these materials are used? Could other materials be used?

If you were to design your own skyscraper, what shape would your skyscraper be? Would it be an office block or full of homes? Would it be in the middle of a city or in the countryside? Why do you think there are no skyscrapers in the country?

What are the advantages and disadvantages of building skyscrapers close together in cities? How do the people who work in them affect traffic and public transportation?

# Useful websites

www.skyscraper.org
The skyscraper museum has great pictures and information on the tallest buildings. Click on "cool stuff for kids" for further information.

http://skyscraperpage.com/diagrams
Diagrams of the world's tallest buildings—including some not yet built.

*Website information is correct at time of going to press. However, the publishers cannot accept liability for any information or links found on third-party websites.*

# Index